THUNDER
OF THE
GODS

OTHER BOOKS
BY DOROTHY HOSFORD

BY HIS OWN MIGHT:
The Battles of Beowulf

SONS OF THE VOLSUNGS

THUNDER
OF THE
GODS

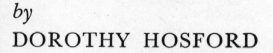

by
DOROTHY HOSFORD

illustrated by
CLAIRE & GEORGE LOUDEN

HENRY HOLT AND COMPANY · NEW YORK

TO
MARY,
THOMAS,
AND
JEAN MARGARET BOYD

CONTENTS

THUNDER
OF THE
GODS

1

THE WORLD OF THE GODS

LONG AGO, in the early days of the world, the gods
of the Norsemen lived in a beautiful city called
Asgard. It stood on a high plain, on top of a lofty
mountain, in the very center of the universe. Its
towers and battlements shone among the clouds.
Odin, the strong and wise father of the gods, had
built this shining city and here he ruled over gods
and men. Odin was called All-Father because he was
the lord and ruler of all. His wife was named Frigg.
She was queen among the goddesses.

Many great palaces and halls rose in Asgard. One
belonged to Odin. In this hall Odin had a high seat

from which he could look out over the whole world. He looked across the highest mountains and into deep valleys and beyond the distant seas, and saw all that took place among men. He watched men plowing their fields and building their houses and fighting their wars.

Odin could look even beyond the realm of men to the dark edges of the world where the giants or Jotuns lived. Their land, which was called Jotunheim, was dark and gloomy, with great mountains and strange valleys. The Frost-Giants and Hill-Giants fought an unceasing war against the gods. The gods wished men well and strove to make life fair and good. But the giants loved evil and destruction. They wished to bring disaster to the whole world of gods and men.

A race of very small creatures also lived in the world, in caves deep beneath the mountains. They were called dwarfs. They were skillful craftsmen and could make every kind of remarkable thing. But they were not always friendly to the gods or to men. There was also a race of lesser deities, called the Vanir, who helped the gods. The winds and the sea and the rain were in their keeping.

Odin looked out from his high seat over all this world and those who lived in it. He had two ravens named Hugin and Munin, which in our language would be Thought and Memory. Each day they flew out over the earth and returned at nightfall to perch on his shoulders and tell what they had seen. In this way Odin gained much knowledge. And often Odin left Asgard and went himself among men.

Thor, the mighty god of thunder, was the son of Odin. He was tall and broad and of great strength. He had a red beard and a hasty temper. When Thor was angered he was terrible in his wrath and all feared him. But he was blunt and honest in his ways and for the most part good-natured and kindly. He waged a constant war against the giants and they knew to their sorrow his prowess as a fighter.

Thor owned a chariot drawn by two goats. When he rode forth the hills trembled, the lightning flashed, and the thunder rolled across the sky. Thor's goats had a remarkable virtue. They could always provide food, no matter into what waste and distant lands his journeys took him. Thor would cook the goats for his supper. He carefully saved the skins and the bones, and in the morning the goats were made whole again. Thor's most priceless possession was his hammer. When he hurled it at a foe, the hammer would always return to his hand. It served him well in his battles against the giants. Many adventures might have turned out differently had it not been for Thor's hammer. He wore iron gauntlets when he hurled it. Thor also possessed a belt of strength. When it was buckled on, the god's strength was doubled. With these possessions and his own great might and courage, Thor overcame all who withstood him—though that is not to say that he had always an easy victory.

Many gods and goddesses lived in Asgard. There was only one among them who did not desire to bring beauty and healing to the world, and to make the ways of men pleasant and prosperous. This was Loki. He came from the race of the giants, though he now lived among the gods and was the foster-brother of Odin. He was pleasing to look upon and beguiling in his ways. But in his heart he loved evil and malice, and the gods learned to their sorrow how little they could trust him.

Also there lived in Asgard a mighty army of heroes. Odin chose the bravest from all who had died on the field of battle. He sent the Valkyries, beautiful maidens mounted on swift steeds, to bear the fallen warriors from the world of men to Asgard. There they remained with the gods. It was the favorite pastime of the heroes to fight battles among themselves each day. Though they might be wounded in the fighting, they were always strong and sound when night came and eager to enjoy the feasts which Odin gave in their honor.

The feasts were held in the great banquet hall called Valhalla. This hall had five hundred and forty portals and through each of these eight hundred warriors could march abreast. The roof of Valhalla rose so high that one could not easily make out the top of it. It was laid with golden shields and glittered in the sunlight. Outside of Valhalla stood the shining grove of Glaser. The leaves of its trees were red gold.

Odin sat on his high seat at the head of the feasts, with his ravens on his shoulders and two wolves at his feet. He wore a blue-gray mantle, the color of sky and clouds, and wings of gold shone on his helmet. Odin drank only wine, which was both food and drink to him. The heroes drank ale and mead which was served to them by the Valkyries. There was never lack of food or drink in Valhalla, no matter how great the company.

So the days passed in Asgard, in adventure and battle, feasting and merriment. Wondrous tales are told of this ancient time, of Odin's journeys and Thor's battles with the giants, of all that happened among the gods. Yet there had been a time in the world when neither Asgard nor the gods were in existence, and there was yet to come a time when all should end.

2

IN THE BEGINNING

THE CITY OF ASGARD did not always shine forth in heaven, with its glittering roofs and towers rising above the clouds and the gods walking its broad roads.

There was a time when there was nothing; neither sea nor land nor sky. No cool waves washed the sandy shores; no grass grew anywhere. Nor had the sun and the moon and the stars yet found their places. All was a great void, a wide abyss. On one side of the abyss was a region of fire and heat called Muspellheim. On the other side was a region of icy frosts and mists called Niflheim. The breath of heat met the frost so that it melted and dripped. Life was quickened from the drops and slowly became a man's form. That man was called Ymir, and from him came all the races of the giants. There also sprang from the melting frost the cow called Audhumla, whose milk nourished the giant Ymir.

The cow licked the blocks of ice, which were salty. The first day that she licked the ice, there came forth from the blocks a man's hair. The second day a man's head came forth, and the third day the whole man was there. He was called Buri and he was great and mighty. He had a son who was called Borr. And Borr, in turn, was the father of Odin and Vili and Ve. These three brothers were good and fair to look upon and worthy of honor. From them was born the whole race of the gods.

From the beginning the giants, sons of Ymir, were the enemies of the gods. They loved to do harm. When the giants were many in number, the three gods put Ymir to death. He was so tremendous in size that the river of blood which flowed from his wounds drowned all the other giants, save one called Bergelmir. He fled, with his wife, in a boat. Thus the gods did not succeed in destroying their enemies, for Bergelmir became the father of a new race of giants.

Odin and his brothers took the body of Ymir and from it they made the earth. First they made the land from his flesh. Then they made the sea from his blood and laid it in a ring about the land. From his bones they fashioned mountains. The gods made the dome of heaven from Ymir's skull and set it up over the earth. Under each corner they placed a dwarf, and the names of these were East, West, North, and South. They made clouds from Ymir's brain. Then the gods took glowing embers and sparks from the fiery region of Muspellheim and made light for the heavens, a sun and a moon and stars.

As yet there were no men in the world. One day as the gods walked along the seashore they took up two trees and formed human beings from them.

"I will give them life and spirit," said Odin.

"I will give them knowledge and understanding," said Vili.

"I will give them bodily shape," said Ve, "and the power to see and hear and speak."

The gods named the man Ask and the woman Embla. From them was all mankind created.

The giants continued without ceasing to disturb the gods at their labors, and they soon began to harry the race of men. To protect men the gods built a great fortress encircling the midmost region of the world. They made it from the eyebrows of Ymir. This fortress and all that it contained was given the name of Midgard. It was the domain of man. Beyond its borders, where the sea joined the edge of the world, lay Jotunheim, the land of the giants.

In the very center of the universe, in the highest part, the gods built the city of Asgard. Here the gods and their kindred dwelt. Many tales and wonders are told of it. The way to Asgard lay across the bridge

Bifrost, which we call the rainbow. It was made with cunning and great magic, and its colors shone brightly in the sky. The god Heimdal guarded the bridge. He needed less sleep than a bird and by day or night could see for a hundred leagues. Heimdal could hear the growing of the grass upon the ground and of wool upon the backs of sheep. He was a fit watchman for the gods.

A mighty ash tree rose above Asgard, whose branches spread abroad over the whole world. It was called Yggdrasil, the tree of the universe. The tree had three great roots. One root was in the realm of the gods, the second was among the Frost-Giants, and the third in the depths of Niflheim. Beside the root in Niflheim was a fearful well, deep and dark, and in its depths lay the dreadful serpent Nidhogg. The serpent gnawed continually at the root of the tree, threatening to destroy it.

The tree flourished in spite of the serpent because it was watered daily with the water from Urd's Well. This well lay beside the root of the tree in the realm of the gods. Its waters were so pure that all things which came into it were made as white as the film which lies within an eggshell. Three of the Norns, those sisters who determined the fate of gods and men, lived beside the root. Each day they took water from Urd's Well and sprinkled it over the tree Yggdrasil so that its limbs would not wither or rot.

Two swans also lived beside Urd's Well. In the branches of the tree lived many animals: a wise eagle, four stags, and the little squirrel named Ratatosk. He ran up and down the tree bearing news between the eagle and the serpent.

It was beside Urd's Well that the gods held their assemblies and gathered together to pass judgment. They crossed over by way of the bridge Bifrost. Only Thor did not trouble to use the bridge. In his impatient way he waded the streams with his long strides and arrived before the others.

Another well lay beside the root in the country of the giants. It belonged to the giant Mimir. Wisdom and knowledge were contained in the waters of this well, and Mimir guarded it closely. One day Odin decided to seek out Mimir and ask a drink from his well. Odin set out from Asgard and traveled the long journey to Jotunheim and Mimir's Well.

"O Mimir," asked Odin, "I would gain wisdom from the waters that lie in your well. Will you give me leave to drink of it?"

"How greatly," asked Mimir, "do you desire this wisdom? The price is dear."

"What do you ask?" said Odin.

"If you will leave one of your eyes with me you shall drink of the well," said Mimir. "That is the only price."

And because Odin so greatly desired to be wise he

gave his eye in exchange for a drink from Mimir's Well. Henceforth he had but one eye to view the outward world, but his wisdom taught him to see deep into the hearts of men.

3

THOR GAINS HIS HAMMER

L OKI MADE MUCH TROUBLE for the gods with his evil pranks and his malice. But there was one time his mischief worked for good in the end. Thor might never have owned his wonderful hammer had it not been for Loki. It came about in this way:

Thor had a beautiful wife whose name was Sif. Her hair was long and yellow and shone like gold in the sunlight. Thor was proud of her.

One day, while Sif lay sleeping under the trees where Iduna's apples grew, Loki cut off all her hair. He did it for a prank. When Sif woke and discovered the loss of her beautiful hair, she went weeping to Thor.

"This is the work of that rascal Loki," cried Thor angrily. "I'll break every bone in his body."

He rushed off to look for Loki. It was not long before he found him and seized him.

13

Loki was filled with terror when he saw Thor's anger. He begged for mercy, but Thor would not let him go.

"Wait, O mighty Thor," begged Loki. "Don't punish me and I will get new hair for Sif. I will find hair of real gold that will shine in the sunlight and will grow like other hair."

"How will you do that?" said Thor.

"I will go to the Dark Elves, to the Sons of Ivaldi, and ask them to make the hair for me," said Loki. "They can make every kind of wondrous thing."

Thor gave his consent.

"But remember," he cried, shaking Loki so that his teeth chattered in his head. "If you don't bring back hair that will grow like other hair, I will break every bone in your body. And it must be as long and beautiful as Sif's own hair. Now go."

Loki was only too glad to set out. The dwarfs lived deep within the mountains and he had a long journey to make.

When Loki came to the dwelling place of the Dark Elves they said that they could perform his task. They made the hair, and they made two other gifts as well. They made the spear Gungnir, which became Odin's possession, and they made the magic ship, Skid-bladnir.

On his way home with the gifts Loki met another dwarf named Brock. Loki was feeling pleased with

himself and proud of his success. At once he made a wager with Brock.

"See what I have," cried Loki. "I'll wager my head that your brother Sindri can't make three gifts as precious as these."

Sindri was famed among the dwarfs and Brock knew how great was his brother's skill.

"I'll take that wager," said Brock. "Come with me. We will go to the smithy and we will see what Sindri can make."

Brock explained the wager to his brother and Sindri started the fire in the forge. The flames lit up the far corners of the dwarfs' cave. When it was hot enough Sindri laid within the fire a pig's hide. He handed the bellows to Brock and told him to work them without ceasing until he should return. Then he left the cave.

As soon as Sindri had gone Loki changed himself into a huge fly. He lit upon Brock's hand and stung him. But Brock kept the bellows working and did not let go.

When Sindri returned he took the work out of the fire. It was a boar, a wild pig with mane and bristles of gold.

Then Sindri placed gold in the fire and bade Brock work the bellows as before. This time the fly settled on Brock's neck and stung twice as hard. But Brock did not let go of the bellows. When Sindri returned he took out of the fire the golden ring which is called Draupnir.

For the third gift Sindri placed iron in the fire. "Keep the bellows going, Brock, or all will be spoiled," said Sindri, as he left the smithy.

This was Loki's last chance and the fly settled between Brock's eyes and stung his eyelids so hard that the blood ran down. The pain and the blood blinded him. Brock had to pause to sweep the fly away. He let go of the bellows with one hand and only for an instant. But the fire died down.

At that moment Sindri returned and said that what was in the hearth had come near to being spoiled. He took the work out of the fire and it was a hammer.

Sindri gave the three gifts to Brock. "Take these to

the gods," he said, "and see whose gifts will win the wager."

Loki and Brock set off for Asgard, the home of the gods, each bearing his gifts. The gods were called together and met in the great council hall named Gladsheim. They took their places on the high seats. It was agreed that Odin and Thor and Frey should decide whose gifts were best.

Loki presented his gifts first. He gave Thor the golden hair for Sif, to Odin he gave the spear Gungnir, and to Frey the ship Skidbladnir, telling the virtues of each. As soon as it was placed upon Sif's head the hair would grow like other hair. The spear Gungnir would never fall short of its mark; and the ship Skidbladnir would always find favoring winds, no matter in what direction it was set. Yet it could be folded like a napkin and placed in Frey's pocket, if he so wished.

Then Brock offered his gifts. He gave to Odin the golden ring which is called Draupnir.

"Every ninth night eight other rings like itself will drop from it," said Brock.

He gave the boar, which was called Gold-Mane, to Frey.

"No horse can run through the air or over the sea with such swiftness," said Brock. "And you can always find your way by the light which shines from its mane and bristles of gold, no matter how black and dark the night may be."

Brock gave the hammer to Thor.

"The name of the hammer is Mjollnir," he told Thor. "With it you can strike as hard a blow as you please at whatever comes in your way. You can hurl it as far as you like, and it will always find its mark and return to your hand. Yet, if you wish, you can make the hammer small and put it in your pocket."

The hammer had only one fault, though Brock did not mention that. The handle was a little short. That was because Loki had caused Brock to drop the bellows.

Odin and Thor and Frey held a council. They decided that Brock's gifts were best, for Thor's hammer was the most valuable gift of all. This was just the weapon the gods needed in their wars against the Frost-Giants. The giants had better beware. Now Thor could hurl his mighty hammer at them and catch it again in his hand.

Odin rose to his feet and announced to all that Brock had won the wager.

Brock immediately demanded Loki's head.

"What good is my head to you?" cried Loki. "I will give you a great sum of gold for a ransom. You will be the richest of all the dwarfs."

Dwarfs love gold, but Brock would have none of it, and said that Loki must keep to the terms of his bargain.

"Then catch me if you can!" cried Loki.

In an instant he was far off, for he had on the shoes which would carry him through air and over water in the twinkling of an eye.

Brock begged Thor to catch Loki. Thor was still angry with Loki and willing enough to do so. Thor asked Frey to lend him the boar Gold-Mane. He leapt on the boar's back and away he went through the air. Before long he had brought Loki back to Asgard.

Brock was ready to cut off his head, but Loki cried: "My head, yes! But not an inch of my neck. I did not wager my neck."

How could Brock cut off Loki's head without touching his neck? Brock had to let it go at that.

"If I had my brother's awl I would sew your mischief-speaking lips together," he cried out in anger.

No sooner had he spoken than the awl was there and of itself pierced Loki's lips. Then Brock sewed them together with a thong. Not that it troubled Loki much, for when Brock was gone he ripped out the thongs.

Loki, as usual, got off with little punishment. But the gods were much richer for their new gifts.

4

THE BUILDING OF
THE FORTRESS WALL

T HIS IS A STORY about the early days of the gods,
when they first lived in Asgard. They had already created Midgard for men to live in and the
mighty hall of Valhalla had been built.

One day a certain stonemason came to the gods
and offered to build them a fortress wall so strong
that no one could overthrow it.

"Within it you would always be safe from the
Frost-Giants and the Hill-Giants, even if they should
break into Midgard," said the mason. "Nothing could
overcome you."

The only difficulty was that for his wages the mason demanded that the goddess Freyja be given to
him in marriage, and he wanted the sun and the
moon as well.

The gods took counsel together. Thor was not present, for at this time he was away in the east fighting

trolls. The gods made a bargain with the builder that he should have what he demanded, but only on condition that he could build the wall in one winter.

"If, when the first day of summer comes, a single stone has not been laid you will forfeit your wages," said Odin. "And no man is to help you in the work."

Then the man asked if he might have the help of his horse, called Svadilfari, to draw stones for him. Loki urged that the gods grant this request, and it was granted.

On the first day of winter the mason set to work. At night he hauled stones with the help of his horse. The gods marveled at the great size of the rocks the stallion could draw, and he did half again as much work as the mason. In the daytime the workman piled the stones with such surprising strength and speed that the gods saw he was no ordinary builder.

The gods could not set aside their bargain, for they had given their pledge. The mason had made certain of that for it seemed unsafe to him to be among the gods without a pledge of peace, especially if Thor should come home from his journeying.

As the winter drew to an end the fortress was almost completed. It towered so high and strong that nothing could have overthrown it. When there were only three days left until summer nothing remained to be finished but the gate of the stronghold.

The gods were greatly disturbed. They sat in their judgment seats and held counsel together, seeking some way by which they could escape from their unwise bargain.

"Who advised that we should give up Freyja?" they asked one another, "or darken the air and the heavens by taking away the sun and the moon?"

The gods agreed that whoever had counseled this had given evil advice, and they remembered that it was Loki who had urged it. They declared Loki deserved a wretched death and they threatened him with violence unless he could think of a way to outwit the mason.

"You were so ready to agree to his bargains," said the gods to Loki. "Now see what you can do to match his wits."

"I give you my oath," said Loki, frightened at the anger of the gods, "I give you my oath that the fortress will not be finished in time, no matter what it costs me."

"Very well," said Odin. "See that you keep your word."

That same evening as the mason drove forth to get rocks, a young mare suddenly ran out of the forest and began to neigh. Then she bounded away into the woods again. The giant's horse, in his eagerness to follow the mare, broke his traces and bolted. The mare, who was Loki in disguise, led the stallion

deeper and deeper into the forest. The two horses galloped happily through the wood, and the mason spent
the whole night in vain pursuit of them.

In the morning not a stone had been added to the
gate of the fortress wall. When the builder saw that
his work would not be finished, he fell into a wild fury
and assumed his true shape. Now the gods saw for
certain it was one of the Hill-Giants who had come
among them. They no longer felt bound by their
oaths and straightway sent for Thor.

Thor crossed the mountains and valleys and rivers
with great strides. When he arrived the giant was
threatening to destroy all of Asgard. But Thor ended
his boastings. With one blow of his mighty hammer
he crushed the giant's skull. Thor paid the mason's
wages, but not with the sun and the moon.

5

THOR'S UNLUCKY JOURNEY

THOR, THE GOD OF THUNDER, was indeed one of the mightiest of the gods. His battles against the Frost-Giants were many. They knew to their sorrow how great he was. Yet it cannot be said that Thor was victor in all his encounters with the giants. There was one adventure in which he was not so lucky.

One day Thor started off in his chariot, driving his goats. Loki went with him. Toward the end of the day they came to the house of a farmer and decided to stay there for the night. Thor's goats could always provide a meal for him. Thor slaughtered his goats and skinned them and had them cooked for supper. He invited the farmer and his wife and their son and daughter to share the meal. The name of the son was Thjalfi and the daughter was named Roskva. Thor told the farmer and his family to throw all the bones down on the skins of the goats, when they had finished their meal. The hides were spread out on the ground a little way from the fire. They did as they were told, except Thjalfi, who was somewhat greedy. He broke one of the bones to get at the sweet-tasting marrow.

In the morning Thor rose. He went over to the goatskins spread on the ground. When he raised his hammer high over the bones the goats sprang to life again. They were just as before except that one of them limped on a hind leg. When Thor saw this he knew someone had disobeyed him and had broken a thigh bone. His brows grew dark with anger and he gripped the handle of his hammer so fiercely that his knuckles grew white. The countryman and his family were terrified when they saw Thor's wrath.

"Have mercy, O Thor," they cried, "we will pay you for the harm we have done. We will give you our house and our cattle and our land. We will give all we own. Have mercy on us, O Mighty One."

When Thor saw how frightened they were he forgot his anger. As payment he agreed to take the son and daughter of the countryman into his service. Thjalfi and Roskva have ever since been with Thor.

They started off again on their journey, leaving the goats behind. They walked until they came to the sea. They waded right through the sea and up to the shore on the other side. In a little while they reached a dark forest and all day they traveled through it. Thjalfi, who was swift-footed beyond all other men, carried Thor's wallet in which were the provisions for the journey. This was not country in which much could be found along the way.

As it grew dark they looked about for a place to spend the night. They found a house with a wide door that stood open the whole length of the house. The house was dark and quiet and they decided to take shelter here for the night. They went in and settled themselves to sleep.

About midnight they heard a great noise. The earth trembled as from an earthquake. They looked about for some place to hide themselves and discovered a smaller doorway leading into a side room. Loki and Thjalfi and Roskva hid themselves in the farthest corner of this room, but Thor sat in the doorway, with his hammer in his hand, ready to meet the danger.

When the light of morning came they all went outside. Roskva began to prepare breakfast. Thor said that he would walk about and have a look at things. A little way off he came upon a huge giant stretched out asleep on the ground. He was snoring mightily and the earth shook beneath him. Then Thor knew what the rumbling and the roaring in the night had been. Thor buckled on his belt of strength, but just at that moment the giant woke and sat up. It is said that

Thor, for once in his life, had no desire to strike a blow.

Instead he asked the giant what his name was. "I am called Skrymir," said the giant, "but I have no need to ask your name. I know well that you are Asa-Thor. But what have you done with my glove?"

As he spoke he stooped and picked up a great glove lying at some distance on the ground. This was what Thor and the others had mistaken in the dark for a house. The smaller doorway into the side room was the opening into the thumb.

"Shall we travel together?" said the giant.

Thor agreed. First they had breakfast, each party eating from its own provisions.

Then Skrymir suggested that they put all the food into one sack. Thor agreed. So Skrymir put Thor's wallet into his sack. He tied the mouth of the sack and flung it over his shoulder.

They started on their journey. Skrymir strode ahead of them with such long strides that it was not easy to keep up with him. They traveled all day. When night came Skrymir found them a place to rest under a wide-spreading oak tree. He flung the sack from his shoulder to the ground.

"Now I am going to sleep," said Skrymir. "You can take your supper from the sack if you like." He lay down a little way off and at once was fast asleep.

The others were hungry. Thor began to untie the

sack so they might have food. Though he pulled and turned and twisted the rope, the knot would not loosen at all. The more Thor struggled, the angrier he grew. Suddenly he seized his hammer with both hands. He went over to where Skrymir lay and dealt him a blow on the head.

Skrymir woke up and said: "What was that? Did a leaf fall on me? Have you had your supper, Thor?"

Thor said they had and were getting ready to sleep. Then they went under another oak and prepared to rest, but they did not feel very safe.

About midnight Thor heard Skrymir snoring so that the woods shook with the sound. He went to where the giant lay and flourishing his hammer above his head, he brought it down with such force that the giant's skull was dented.

Skrymir woke up. "Now what is that?" he said. "Has an acorn fallen on me? How is it with you, Thor?"

Thor said that it was only midnight and there was still time for sleeping.

"I just happened to waken," said Thor. Then he went back to his place speedily.

Skrymir stretched out again. Thor lay quiet, but he was not asleep. He thought that if he could give Skrymir just one more blow, the giant would not see day again. Just before dawn Thor heard Skrymir snoring. Running to where he lay, Thor struck him such a mighty blow on the temple that the hammer sank into the skull up to its handle.

But Skrymir sat up and stroked his cheek. "Did a twig fall on my face? Are you awake, Thor? It is almost day, and time we were on our way."

They prepared to start their journey. Then Skrymir said: "You have no long way to go now to reach the home of the giants. But let me give you a word of advice: don't brag too much of your prowess there, for Utgard-Loki and his men have little patience with the boasting of such small fellows as you. Perhaps it would be wiser if you did not go at all. Yet if you are determined to keep on your journey, take the way to the east. My road lies north, to those mountains you see beyond you."

Skrymir flung the sack of food over his shoulder and was gone without another word. It has never been said that the others were sorry to see him go.

Thor and his companions traveled all morning. About noon they caught sight of a great castle standing in the middle of a plain. The top of it was so high that they had to bend their heads back before they could see it. The gate to the castle was locked. Thor went up to it and tried to open it, but could not move it. So they crept in between the bars. They saw before them a huge hall and went toward it. The door was open and they went inside.

There they saw many men sitting about on benches and none of them could be called small men. Utgard-Loki, king of the giants, was among them. They went before him and saluted him. He took his time to look them over, laughing at them scornfully through his teeth.

"There is no need to ask news of a long journey," said Utgard-Loki. "Is this stripling Asa-Thor? Or am I wrong? Tell us in what you are skilled, you and your fellows. For no one is allowed to remain among us who cannot do some thing better than other men."

Loki, who was standing behind the others, spoke up. "There is one thing I am ready to wager at once, and that is that I can eat faster than anyone here."

"We shall soon find out," answered Utgard-Loki. Then he shouted for a man named Logi to come to the center of the hall to try his skill with Loki. A great trencher of food was brought and placed upon the floor. Loki and Logi sat down at each end of it and began to eat with all their might. They met in the middle of the trencher. Loki had eaten all the meat from the bones, but Logi had consumed the meat and the bones and the trencher as well. So Loki was beaten at this game.

"What is that young man able to do?" asked Utgard-Loki, pointing to Thjalfi.

"I am willing to try a race with someone," answered Thjalfi.

"You will need to be swift of foot," said Utgard-Loki.

They all went outside. The level plain was a good place for running a race. Utgard-Loki called a small fellow named Hugi. He told him to run against Thjalfi.

They started. Hugi was far enough ahead that he met Thjalfi as he turned back at the end of the course.

"You will have to stretch your legs more than that, Thjalfi, if you are to win," said Utgard-Loki. "Yet it is true that never have men come here who could run so well."

When they ran the second trial Hugi was so far ahead that when he turned back at the end of the course, Thjalfi had still the length of a bow shot to run.

"Well run," said Utgard-Loki, "but I cannot think that Thjalfi will win if you should run a third time."

Thjalfi ran the third time with all his might, and he was the swiftest of men. Yet Hugi had come to the end of the course and turned back before Thjalfi had reached the middle of it.

All agreed that Hugi had won the race.

Then they went inside the hall and Utgard-Loki asked Thor in what way he would try his skill. "We have heard great things of your prowess, Thor," said he.

"I will drink with anyone who cares to drink," said Thor.

"Very good," said Utgard-Loki. He called his serving boy to bring the great horn from which the henchmen sometimes drank.

"It is considered a good drink if you can empty this horn at one draught," said Utgard-Loki. "Some among us must drink twice, but there is not any man here who cannot drain it in three draughts."

Thor took the horn. He thought it not too large, though it seemed somewhat long. Thor was thirsty. He put the horn to his lips and took a long, deep draught. He thought to himself that he would not have to take more than one drink. But when he had to stop for breath and put the horn down he saw, to his surprise, that there was but little less in it than there had been before.

"Well," said Utgard-Loki, "that was a pretty good drink. But if anyone had told me that Asa-Thor could not drink more than this I would not have believed it. No doubt you will drain it this time."

Thor answered nothing. He put his mouth to the horn again and drank as long as he could hold his breath. When he paused it seemed to him that it had gone down even less than before. Yet at least one could now tilt the horn a little without spilling it.

"Well," said Utgard-Loki, "can you finish that in one more draught? It seems to me that you have perhaps left overmuch for the last drink. It cannot be said that you are as great here among us as you are among the gods, unless you are more skilled in other games than in this."

Thor grew angry. He put the horn to his mouth and drank with all his might. He struggled with it and drank as long as he could, but when he had to put the horn down again it was still almost full. Yet it could be said that a little space had been made in it. But Thor would drink no more.

"It can be plainly seen that you are not so great as we thought you were," said Utgard-Loki. "Will you try your skill at other games, since you won no praise in this one?"

"I will risk it," said Thor. "Yet I know that at home among the gods my drink would not have seemed so little."

"We have a game among us that does not amount to much," said Utgard-Loki. "Our young boys like to play it. It is to lift my cat from the floor. Indeed I would not have dared to mention it had I not seen that Asa-Thor is by no means as great as we thought he was."

There leaped forth upon the hall floor a large gray cat. Thor put one hand down under the middle of its body and stretched upward. But the more he stretched the more the cat arched its back. Though he stretched as high as he could the cat only lifted one foot off the floor. And Thor had to give up that game.

"The game went just as I thought it would," said Utgard-Loki. "The cat is very great, and Thor is low and little beside the huge men who are here with us."

"Call me little if you will," cried Thor, "but let anyone here come and wrestle with me. For now I am angry."

"I see no man here who would not hold it a disgrace to wrestle with you," said Utgard-Loki looking about the benches. "Let my old nurse, Elli, be called. Thor can wrestle with her if he wishes. She has thrown men who have seemed to me no less strong than Thor."

There appeared an old woman, bent with age. Thor grappled with her, but the more he struggled the firmer she stood. He could in no way throw her. She began to try some tricks of her own and Thor tottered. Then Thor went down upon one knee.

Utgard-Loki came up and bade them cease wrestling. "There is no need now," said he, "for Thor to challenge any of my men."

It was now toward evening. Utgard-Loki showed Thor and his companions to a seat at one of the benches. They remained throughout the night and were treated with great hospitality.

When morning came Thor and the others rose and made ready to leave. Utgard-Loki himself came into the hall. He ordered a table set for them with every kind of food and drink. When they had eaten, he went to see them on their way. As they were about to part, Utgard-Loki said:

"What think you, Thor, of this journey? Have you met any man mightier than yourself?"

"What I have done here will gain me small praise," answered Thor. "What troubles me most is that you will think me a man of little might."

"Now that you are out of the castle, I will tell you something," said Utgard-Loki. "If I live and prevail, Thor, you will never come into it again. This I know, by my troth, you should never have come into it at all had I known what strength you had! You nearly had us all in great peril."

Utgard-Loki went on speaking: "I have tricked you, Thor. It was I whom you met in the wood. I tied the sack of food with troll-iron, so that you could not undo it. When you went to smite me with the hammer I brought a mountain between us, though you could not see it. Otherwise the first blow would have slain me. Do you see that mountain with the three valleys, one deeper than the others? Those are the marks of your blows.

"It was the same with the games you played against my henchmen," continued Utgard-Loki. "There you were tricked, too. Loki was hungry and he ate ravenously, but he who was called Logi was Fire and he devoured the trencher as well as the meat. Thjalfi ran the race with Hugi, who is Thought—and how could Thjalfi outrun Thought?"

"And how did you trick *me*, Utgard-Loki?" said Thor.

"When you drank from the horn, Thor, it seemed to you to go down slowly. But that was a wonder I could hardly believe even when I saw. For the other end of the horn was in the sea itself, though you knew it not. When you look at the sea you will notice how the water has drawn back. From hence we shall call that the Ebb Tide.

"And my gray cat was not as it appeared to be. It was the Midgard Serpent itself which is twined about the whole earth. It was the same with the wrestling match. It was a marvel that you withstood so long and bent only one knee. You struggled with Old Age and all men must give in to Old Age at last.

"And now," said Utgard-Loki, "it is best that we part. It will be better for us both if you come not here again. I will defend my castle with every trick I know, so that you shall get no power over me."

When Thor knew he had been tricked, he seized his hammer and would have hurled it at Utgard-Loki. But the giant had disappeared. Thor turned toward the castle, thinking to crush it with a blow from the hammer. It was gone also. There was nothing before them but the green and level plain.

So Thor turned back, with the others, and made his way to Thrudvang, his own realm. Already his thoughts were busy as to how he might be revenged.

"One day," said Thor to himself, "I will seek out the Midgard Serpent. We shall see if I be 'little and low.'"

6

THOR'S VISIT TO HYMIR

EVERY YEAR the gods gathered together for a great feast in the hall of Aegir, who was lord of the sea. It was at this feast that Thor complained that he could not get enough to drink.

"Well," said Aegir, "that is because I have no kettle large enough to brew ale for all the gods at once. You should be able to find me such a kettle."

None of the gods knew where there was a kettle as large as that, nor had they ever heard of one. Then Tyr, the god of war, spoke up:

"My fierce father, the giant Hymir, owns such a kettle. It is a mighty vessel. A mile deep it is."

"Would there be any way," asked Thor, "that we might win this kettle?"

"Yes," answered Tyr, "I think we might win it if we use great cunning."

Thor and Tyr set forth at once for Jotunheim.

They drove Thor's chariot until they came to the house of a man named Egil. There they left the goats and went the rest of the way on foot.

After a considerable journey they reached the home of the giant. Tyr's mother welcomed them and

gave them ale to quench their thirst. When they had refreshed themselves she pointed out eight large kettles which hung from a beam.

"I will hide you behind those kettles," she said. "Hymir is not always friendly toward visitors."

It was late when the great giant returned from his hunting. He was covered with snow and the icicles which hung from his frosty beard made a tinkling sound.

His wife greeted him with fair words: "A pleasant

evening to you, Hymir. May your thoughts be kind. Our son, for whom we have waited so long, has come. He has brought with him his friend Thor. There they wait beneath the gable, behind those kettles."

The giant turned angrily toward the place where Thor and Tyr were hiding. His glance was so fierce that the pillar splintered and the mighty beam above them broke. The kettles clattered to the floor. Only one of them, harder and stronger than the others, remained whole. The rest broke in pieces.

Then Thor and Tyr came forth. The giant and the god gazed upon each other. Hymir was not pleased to see the mighty Thor within his household, but even a giant offers food to his guests. Hymir ordered three steers to be brought and cooked for supper. Thor ate two of the steers. Even to Hymir this seemed a large meal indeed.

"We shall have to seek more food tomorrow and see if we can find something really worth eating," he said crossly.

In the morning when Hymir prepared to go fishing Thor asked if he might go. Hymir said yes and Thor asked what he should use for bait. The giant was not in a good temper.

"Why not go to the herd, you slayer of giants, and see what bait you can find there," he answered.

Thor went to the field where Hymir's cattle were

grazing. He twisted the head from the largest bull of all.

Hymir was amazed when he saw Thor return with his bait.

"One never knows what you will do," he grumbled, "save when you sit still."

Thor sat down in the stern seat as Hymir shoved out the boat. Thor took up two oars and began to row and it seemed to Hymir that they made rapid progress. Hymir rowed forward in the bow and the boat sped through the water.

Then Hymir put down his oars and said they had arrived at the fishing banks where he was accustomed to anchor.

"Oh," said Thor, "we will go much farther than this." He pulled the oars sharply and the boat shot ahead.

Then Hymir said again that they had come so far that it was perilous to go farther.

"The Midgard Serpent lies in these depths," cried Hymir.

"There is no need to stop yet," said Thor, and he kept on rowing. But Hymir was sore afraid.

After a while Thor laid aside the oars and made ready a strong fishing line. The hook was no less large and strong. Hymir began to fish for whales and caught two almost at once. Thor put the head of the ox on his hook and cast it overboard with such strength that it went straight to the bottom of the sea. Thor was not trying to catch whales, but the Midgard Serpent itself.

Now the Midgard Serpent, lying in the depths of the sea, snapped at the ox head which Thor had thrown into the water. The hook caught in its jaw. When the serpent felt the hook it gave a mighty leap and pulled the line so fiercely and suddenly that both Thor's fists crashed against the gunwale of the boat. The pain made Thor angry and he summoned all his strength. He braced his feet so strongly that they went through the boat and down to the floor of the sea.

With a great heave of the line Thor drew the serpent up to the gunwale of the boat. It was a fearful sight. Thor flashed fiery glances at the serpent. The serpent, snorting venom, lashed the waters so that all the monsters of the deep trembled. The rocks resounded and the very earth itself was shaken. Hymir grew yellow with fear. Thor lifted his hammer to strike. At that moment the frightened giant fumbled for his fishing knife and hacked off Thor's line at the gunwale. The serpent sank into the sea.

Thor was furious. With one blow of his fist he knocked Hymir headfirst into the water, so that the soles of his feet were uppermost. Then Thor reached over and dragged him into the boat again.

Unhappily Thor rowed back to land, while Hymir sat in the stern without speaking a word.

By the time they reached land Hymir had recovered a little. Once more he tried to humble Thor, this time by testing his strength.

"Will you," said Hymir, "make fast the boat or will you carry the whales to the house?" A steep, wooded gorge lay between the shore and the house.

Thor did not answer but stooped down and drew the boat ashore with one hand. He did not even bother to empty the water out of it. He picked up the boat and the oars and the bailing dipper, and the whales as well. He carried them to the giant's house as though it were no task at all.

Hymir was not yet satisfied. He was a stubborn giant.

"I will call no one truly strong," he said, when they were seated at supper, "no matter how stoutly he rows, or what burdens he carries, unless he can break this beaker." And he handed Thor a drinking cup.

Thor took the cup and hurled it against one of the stone pillars of the house. The pillar was shattered but the cup remained whole.

Then the wife of Hymir whispered to Thor: "Throw it against the skull of Hymir, for it is harder than glass ever was."

Thor rose and with all his strength hurled the cup against Hymir's forehead. Hymir was not hurt but the cup was broken into pieces.

The giant lamented the loss of his wine cup. But there was nothing more he could ask of Thor.

"You can have the kettle if you can carry it out of the house," he said.

First Tyr tried to lift it. He used all his strength without being able to move the kettle.

So Thor must try himself. He seized the rim and took so strong a grip that his feet went through the floor. Finally he succeeded in slinging the kettle over his head. It was so large that it covered him and the handles clattered about his heels.

Thor and Tyr hurried off and traveled a great distance before they paused. When they looked back they saw Hymir coming in pursuit with great numbers of giants.

Thor stood where he was and cast the kettle from his shoulders. He swung his hammer over his head and let it fly into the midst of the giants. With one blow he killed them all.

And this was how Thor won the kettle from Hymir. He brought the kettle back to the gods and never again was there lack of ale at Aegir's feasts.

7

HOW ODIN BROUGHT THE MEAD TO ASGARD

In the early days of the world a dispute arose between the gods and the Vanir. A meeting was held to settle the quarrel and as a pledge of peace the gods created a man whom they called Kvasir. They gave him great wisdom, so that he knew the answer to all questions.

Kvasir traveled far and wide over the world sharing his wisdom with men. He taught men all manner of things. His words were gentle and beautiful and fell softly on the ear.

It came about that Kvasir was invited to the dwelling of certain dwarfs. Their names were Fjalar and Galarr. They were crafty and treacherous and loved to do evil. They killed Kvasir and let his blood run into two large crocks and a kettle. The dwarfs blended honey with the blood. They made a mead from this brew which had not only the richness and sweetness of honey, but the wisdom which ran in Kvasir's blood. The mead had this virtue: anyone who drank of it became a poet, bringing songs and beauty to men.

When the dwarfs had slain Kvasir they looked about for new mischief to do. They asked the giant Gilling to visit them and to bring his wife. When Gilling came they took him out upon the sea to fish. When they were well out from land, the dwarfs rowed into a reef and capsized the boat. Gilling was unable to swim and was drowned, but the dwarfs righted their boat and returned to land. They told Gilling's wife that the giant had fallen out of the boat and drowned. She took the news grievously and wept aloud.

"Would it ease your heart," said Fjalar craftily, "if you could look out upon the sea at the spot where Gilling perished?"

The giant's wife said that it would comfort her and prepared to go forth to the sea.

Then Fjalar whispered to his brother to go up over the doorway and when the giant's wife came out to let a millstone fall on her head.

"Her weeping grows wearisome to me," said Fjalar.

His brother did as he was told.

Now the giant Suttung, who was Gilling's son, learned of these things and set out to seek revenge. He was a great and powerful giant. He came to where the dwarfs lived and he carried them out to sea and set them on a reef, over which the sea swept at high tide. The dwarfs begged Suttung to spare their lives.

"Save us and we will give you the precious mead made from Kvasir's blood," cried the dwarfs. "Men and gods would give anything to possess it, for he who drinks of it becomes a poet."

The giant thought that would be a precious thing to own indeed. The ransom was agreed upon and he carried the dwarfs safely to land. Suttung took the mead home and concealed it. He put his daughter Gunlod to keep watch over it.

When all these events came to the knowledge of Odin, he determined to secure the mead for the gods. The gods had created Kvasir. The precious mead brewed from his blood belonged to the gods, not to the giants. Odin told the other gods the purpose of his journey and set forth from Asgard.

He had traveled a long way when he came to a certain field where nine thralls were cutting hay. Odin watched the men working.

"Your scythes seem not oversharp," said he. "I have a good whetstone. Would you like them sharpened?"

"We would like them sharpened," said the thralls.

Odin took his whetstone from his belt and sharpened the scythes. When the thralls began mowing the field again it seemed that their scythes had never cut so well. They asked Odin if he would sell the whetstone.

"It is an excellent stone as you see," said Odin, "and worth a high price."

"We agree to any price," said the thralls. "Pray sell us the stone."

Odin was willing, but since each one clamored for the stone he tossed it into the air for them to catch. All wished to lay their hands upon it at once. They became so entangled that they cut each other's throats with their scythes. All were killed.

Odin then sought a night's lodging with the giant Baugi, who was Suttung's brother. He lived near by and the thralls belonged to him.

Baugi welcomed Odin for the night, and while they sat at supper Baugi lamented the loss of his thralls.

"They were stupid indeed to lose their lives in such fashion," he said, "but they were my only thralls. What will happen to my fields now? I know no way to find new laborers."

"I will do the work of your thralls this summer," said Odin. "I myself can do all that they did."

"Who are you that can do the work of nine men?" said Baugi.

"My name is Bolverk," said Odin. And that was

all he said about himself. The name Bolverk means one who can perform the most difficult tasks.

"But if I do this work for you," continued Bolverk, "I must have one drink of Kvasir's mead. It is your brother Suttung who keeps it."

Baugi declared that Suttung guarded the mead jealously and let no one come near it.

"I have never seen it," said Baugi. "Nevertheless when the summer is over I will go with you to Suttung. We shall see if we can persuade him to let you drink of the mead."

And so the bargain was made. Through the summer Bolverk worked for Baugi and did the work of nine men.

When the summer was over they both set out for Suttung's dwelling.

Baugi told Suttung of his bargain with Bolverk, but Suttung flatly refused them a single drop of the mead. Then Bolverk suggested to Baugi that they try certain wiles and see whether they could find a way to get at the mead. Baugi readily agreed to this.

Suttung had hidden the mead in a huge rocky cave. Gunlod, Suttung's daughter, kept watch over it. Bolverk and Baugi went to the cave. They looked at it from every side and saw that there was no way to make an easy entrance to it.

"The mead is indeed well guarded," said Bolverk, "but I think we can find a means to get at it."

Then Bolverk drew forth from his pocket an auger.

"Take this," he said to Baugi, "and see if you can bore through the rock with it."

Baugi began to bore with the auger. It was hard work cutting through the rock and Baugi grew weary. At length Baugi said he had bored through the rock. But when Bolverk blew into the auger hole the chips flew up in his face.

"I see that you would deceive me, Baugi, if you could," said Bolverk. "The hole has not been bored through the rock or the chips would not fly in my face. Take the auger and bore again."

Baugi set to work once more, but he was angry that he had been unable to deceive Bolverk. After a while Baugi said that he was now through the rock. When Bolverk blew the second time the chips were blown through the hole and Bolverk knew an opening had been made at the other end.

Then Bolverk changed himself into a serpent and crawled into the hole. Baugi wished to be rid of Bolverk and of his bargain, and he tried to pierce the serpent with the auger. But the serpent was already beyond his reach.

Bolverk crawled through the hole to the inside of the cave. There he resumed his true shape. He approached the giant's daughter. Gunlod was lonely, sitting here by herself watching over the mead. She welcomed the guest who greeted her so pleasantly.

And she surmised from his appearance and the strange fashion of his coming that he must be one of the gods.

Odin remained with Gunlod for three days and she was happy in his company. At the end of that time he persuaded her to give him leave to drink three times from the mead. In the first draught he drank every drop out of the kettle, and in the second drink he emptied the first crock, and in the third drink he emptied the last crock.

Then Odin flung open the door of the cave. Changing himself into an eagle he soared into the sky, flying with all speed in the direction of Asgard.

From his dwelling Suttung saw the flight of the eagle from the cave. He guessed what had happened. He also changed himself into an eagle and flew in pursuit of Odin.

Odin flew with such power that it was not long before the golden towers of Asgard came into view. But Suttung also had great strength and he was only a short distance behind Odin.

When the gods saw the two eagles flying they knew it was Odin with Suttung in pursuit. Quickly they set out large crocks. The moment Odin flew over the walls of Asgard he emptied the mead, which he had carried in his mouth, into the crocks.

But so great had been his hurry to escape Suttung that some of the mead had spilled to the ground in his flight. The gods were not concerned with this and let who would gather it up.

Suttung, when he saw Odin wheel across the walls of Asgard, knew he was safe. The precious mead was forever in the possession of the gods. Suttung, to save himself, whirled in the air and flew off speedily toward Jotunheim.

Thus Odin brought the magic gift of Kvasir to the gods. The gods kept it not for themselves, but bestowed it as a gift upon those among men who knew how to value it. They became poets. Gods and men loved to hear their words and the wondrous songs they sang. The drops of mead which spilled to the ground were left to comfort the would-be poets upon earth.

So Kvasir's mead, instead of lying useless in Suttung's cave, brought wonder and joy and beauty to the world.

8

THOR'S HAMMER IS STOLEN

O NE MORNING when Thor awoke he found that his hammer had disappeared. He looked for it everywhere. There was no sign of it in any place and Thor knew then that it had been stolen. He clenched his jaws angrily and his beard quivered with rage. Thor took an oath that he would get his hammer back and have revenge upon the thief.

"The giants have done this," said Thor to himself.

He sought out Loki. "Heed my words, Loki," said Thor. "No one knows, in heaven or on earth, what I am about to tell you. Our hammer is stolen!"

Loki and Thor decided to go to Freyja and ask her help.

"Freyja," said Thor, "my hammer has been stolen. Will you lend me your dress of feathers that Loki may fly through the air and seek news of it?"

"Gladly will I lend it, Thor," said Freyja. "You should have it though it were made of the brightest silver; I would give it to you though it were spun from precious gold."

Loki put on Freyja's feather dress and away he flew across the sky. The feather dress whirred in the wind. Loki flew until he had left the home of the gods far behind. At last he came to the realm of the giants.

He found Thrym, the king of the giants, sitting on a mound with his horses and dogs about him. He was braiding leashes of gold for the dogs. Now and then he would stop to comb a horse's mane.

Thrym saw Loki and spoke to him: "What is the news with Loki? How fare the gods? Why come you alone to the land of the giants?"

"It fares ill with the gods," answered Loki. "Perhaps you know the cause of it. Would you, by any chance, know what has happened to Thor's hammer?"

Thrym laughed. He laughed a great, loud laugh that went rumbling among the mountains like Thor's thunder.

"I have hidden Thor's hammer eight miles deep in the earth," he said. "Thor shall not have it back until I win Freyja for my wife."

Then Loki flew away again. The feather dress whirred in the wind. Soon he had left the home of the giants far behind. At last he reached the realm of the gods.

Thor was waiting for him in the courtyard. "What news, Loki?" he cried. "What news? Have you tidings to tell?"

"I have tidings to tell," said Loki, "and I have trouble to tell also. Thrym has hidden your hammer eight miles deep in the earth. He says no man will find it unless Freyja becomes his bride."

This was not good news to Thor. "Let us ask Freyja," he said. "But I think little will come of it."

Thor and Loki went to Freyja's house and told her what Thrym asked for the return of the hammer.

"Will you put on a bridal veil, Freyja? Loki has found the hammer. Thrym has hidden it eight miles deep in the earth. He will not give it up unless you become his bride. What say you to that, Freyja?"

Thor was right that little would come of it. Freyja, angry they should think of such a thing, sent them forth with scornful words.

"How dare you ask Freyja to become the wife of a giant," she cried. "What would be said of me if I became Thrym's bride? Nay, Thor, you ask too much."

Then the gods and goddesses gathered together in council to find some way to bring Thor's hammer back to Asgard. No one could think what to do. At last Heimdal spoke.

"If Freyja will not go, let Thor go in her place," said Heimdal. "Thrym will not know him if we cover his face with a bridal veil and hang Freyja's necklace about his neck. We can put a woman's dress upon him and let keys hang from his girdle in the fashion of women. He can wear gems upon his breast and a pretty cap upon his head."

The gods laughed to think of Thor in the long garments of a woman. Thor did not laugh. He was angry.

"That I will not do," cried Thor. "I will not go to Thrym with skirts about my legs."

"Would you have the giants keep your hammer?" said Loki. "With your hammer they will be mightier than the gods. The day will soon come when they will destroy the gods and rule in Asgard."

Thor had no answer to this. Most unwillingly he let them dress him as a bride. They put a woman's dress upon him and hung keys at his girdle, as women wear them. They covered his face with a bridal veil and hung Freyja's necklace about his neck. They put a pretty cap upon his head.

"I will go as your serving-maid," said Loki. He, too, dressed as a woman.

Thor's chariot was brought and the goats were harnessed to it. Thor and Loki rode off, swift as the wind. Beneath the wheels of the chariot the mountains burst, earth burned with fire.

When Thrym saw them coming he shouted with delight. He called to the giants to prepare the hall for a feast and to put fresh straw upon the benches.

"I have cattle in my stables with horns of gold," said Thrym to himself. "I have black oxen. Great stores of treasure and jewels are mine. I needed only Freyja to be my wife. Now I shall have everything."

Thrym welcomed Freyja and her serving-maid. When evening was come they all sat down to a great feast in the hall. Thor alone ate a whole ox and eight salmon. He ate all the delicacies that were placed before the women. And he drank three crocks of ale.

Thrym gazed in amazement. "Never did I see bride eat so well, or take such great bites," said he. "Never did I see maiden drink such quantities of mead."

"Freyja has not touched a morsel of food for eight days, so great has been her longing for Thrym," said Loki, the serving-maid.

Then Thrym lifted the corner of the veil for he wished to kiss his bride. But he dropped the veil and shrank back in fright.

"Why are Freyja's eyes so fierce? They burn like flames of fire."

"Freyja has not slept a wink for eight nights, so great has been her longing for Thrym," said the crafty Loki.

Then the giant's sister came forward, as was the custom, and asked for a bridal gift from Freyja.

"If you would have my praise," said she, "give me the gold rings from your fingers."

But Thrym grew impatient. He cried loudly that the hammer should be brought and laid upon the knees of the bride, so that the wedding might take place.

The hammer was brought into the hall. When Thor saw it again his heart laughed within him. As soon as it was laid upon his knees he seized it. With one mighty blow he killed Thrym. Then he struck to the right and to the left and the giants fell before him. He destroyed them all.

At once Thor and Loki harnessed the goats and rode off in Thor's chariot, swift as the wind. It has not been said that any one ever again tried to steal Thor's hammer.

9

THE WINNING OF GERD

FREY WAS the god of weather; he made the sun shine and the rain fall. He brought about the harvests of the fields and gave men prosperity and joy and peace. Frey was a favorite among gods and men; he was fair to look upon and brave in all his deeds.

One day Frey sat in the high seat which belonged to Odin, from whence one could look out over all the world. It was a bold thing for a god to sit in Odin's place, and perhaps the sorrow that lay heavily upon Frey after he had done this deed was Odin's way of reproving him. All turned out well in the end, but for a time Frey was the least happy of the gods.

Frey sat in the high seat and turned his gaze to every corner of the world—to the south and to the east and to the west. As he looked toward the north, in the direction of Jotunheim, he saw a maiden walking toward a great house. As she raised her arm to open the door a brightness shone all about her. It seemed as though the whole earth, and all the air and the sea, were made light. Frey thought he had never seen anyone so fair, and a great longing for her rose in his heart.

He went home full of sadness and did not speak to anyone, nor could he eat or sleep. So great was his sorrow that no man dared speak to him.

Then Frey's father, seeing the strange behavior of his son, sent for Frey's messenger, whose name was Skirnir. He commanded Skirnir to go to Frey and to beg words with him.

"Ask him," said Frey's father, "why he has grown so sad and bitter that he will not speak with men."

"I would rather not go," said Skirnir, "but I will do as you command. I fear Frey will not receive me with kindness."

But Skirnir went directly to Frey and questioned him.

"Why, O Frey," he asked, "are you so sad of countenance and so heavy of heart? Why sit you alone in these halls for days together and speak not with men?"

"How can I tell of a grief so great as mine?" said Frey. "Though the sun rises every morning it lightens not my longing."

"Surely your longing and grief is not so great that you cannot tell it to me," said Skirnir. "We were youths together. Can we not trust each other?"

So Frey told him that he had seen a maiden, fair beyond all others, and that it was for her sake he was so full of grief.

"I looked out over the world," said Frey, "and I saw a maiden who is dear to me above all the maidens of the earth. She was so fair and bright that all the earth was lightened. But she is the daughter of the giant Gymir and none will grant that she shall be my wife."

"If this be so, what will you do?" asked Skirnir.

"You must go, Skirnir, and woo her on my behalf," said Frey. "You must bring her whether her father wills it or not. I shall reward you well."

"Then you must give me your horse that will ride through the dark and fears not the magic, burning flames," answered Skirnir. "And you must give me your sword that of itself will fight the giants."

"Take what you will," said Frey. "I care not what I lose so I win the maiden Gerd."

But Frey was afterward to regret the loss of his faithful sword, which in the heat of battle could strike, if need be, of its own accord. In the fight with the giant Beli he had to use the antlers of a stag to kill his enemy. And in the last battle of the gods Frey had great need of his sword. But now he thought only of winning the maiden he loved and he gave the sword to Skirnir.

Skirnir, riding Frey's horse and carrying his sword, set out for Jotunheim. It was a journey full of perils, but Skirnir urged the horse on through all the dark ways. He loved the horse and was happy that it now belonged to him.

"It is dark without and the way is wild, but together we shall seek the home of the giants," said Skirnir softly. "And we shall come back together, if the terrible giant takes not our lives."

When Skirnir arrived in the land of the giants he rode toward Gymir's realm. A wall of fire marked its boundaries. But Skirnir's horse had no fear of fire and they sped through the flames with ease. Fierce dogs were chained before the gate of Gymir's dwelling. The dogs growled and snarled as Skirnir came toward them.

Skirnir turned and rode to where a herdsman sat on a hill, guarding the giant's cattle.

"Tell me, herdsman, you who sit on this hill and keep watch over all the paths," said Skirnir, "how can I win a word with the maiden who lives within that house? How can I pass the hounds of Gymir there?"

"Have you no care for your life or are you dead already, horseman," answered the herdsman, "that you ride hither and ask this question? There is no way whatever for you to have speech with Gymir's daughter."

"It is better for a man to be bold than to ask idle questions," answered Skirnir. "My life has its appointed end and I will strive until that day comes."

He turned away and his horse's hoofs thundered down the hillside. The giant's daughter heard the noise within the house.

"What noise is that which I hear so loud?" said Gerd. "The ground shakes and the house of Gymir trembles about me."

"There is one without who has leapt from his steed and comes toward the gate," answered the serving-maid.

"Silence the dogs and bid the man come in. Let him drink good mead here within our hall," said Gerd.

"Are you of the elves, or a son of the gods, or come you from the Vanir," said Gerd, when Skirnir had come within the house. "How have you ridden alone through the leaping flames and come within sight of our dwelling?"

"I am not of the elves, nor a child of the gods, nor of the Vanir. Yet I came alone through the leaping flames to reach your dwelling," answered Skirnir. "I have words to speak to you, Gerd."

"Speak them then," said Gerd.

"Frey has sent me to ask if you will be his bride,"

said Skirnir, holding forth his hands. "Here are eleven apples, all of gold. These shall be yours, Gerd, if you will plight your troth to Frey."

"I will take those apples for no man's sake," answered Gerd. "Nor shall I ever be the bride of Frey."

"Here is a ring most wondrous fair," said Skirnir. "Long have the gods cherished it. Great and strange are its powers."

"The gods may prize it, but I need it not," answered Gerd. "There is no lack of golden rings in my father's house."

Then said Skirnir: "Look on this keen bright sword that I hold in my hand. Unless you do my will I shall strike your head from your shoulders."

"Not for any man's sake will I be frightened by threats," Gerd answered proudly. "If my father Gymir finds you here he will fight you gladly."

"The sword in my hand," said Skirnir, "will slay your father. No giant can withstand its strength."

Then, since all other means had failed, Skirnir began to chant these runes:

> You shall go where never again
> The sons of men will see you,
> You shall sit alone on the eagle's hill
> And gaze on the gates of Hela.
>
> Changed your shape and fearful to see,
> My doom will be upon you,

My doom of heavy heart and double sorrow,
Grief shall you get instead of gladness.

The anger of Odin will you bear,
Frey shall be your foe,
Most evil maid, for yourself have you won
The magic wrath of the gods.

I say thee a charm and three runes with it,
Longing and sadness and pain,
But what I have said I may yet unsay
If I find a reason for it.

Skirnir lifted a magic wand above Gerd's head as he spoke these strange and bitter words. A change came over the maiden.

Gerd was not lured by the apples of the gods, nor by the magic ring, nor did she fear the edge of Skirnir's sword. But the spell of the runes and the power of Skirnir's wand moved her heart. She smiled on Skirnir.

"Be welcome here, Frey's messenger, and drink with me a cup of the giant's mead," said Gerd. "I give my promise gladly, though I did not think ever to love one of the race of the gods."

Then Skirnir answered: "I must know your will truly before I ride homeward with my tidings. How soon will you meet the mighty son of Njorth?"

"There is the forest of Barri which we both know well," said Gerd. "It is a forest fair and still. Nine nights from now will I be there and plight my troth with Frey."

Skirnir rode home. Frey was waiting his return. He caught the bridle of Skirnir's horse.

"Tell me quickly, Skirnir," he cried. "Tell me from where you sit what tidings you bring from the giant's dwelling. Is it news to make me glad?"

"There is the forest of Barri which we both know well," answered Skirnir. "It is a forest fair and still. Nine nights from now will Gerd be there and plight her troth to you."

"Long is one night; longer are two. How shall I wait even three?" said Frey. "Often a month has seemed less long than half a night seems now."

And so it was that Frey won the maiden he loved. Gerd became the wife of Frey and they lived long years in happiness together. Though the time was to come, in the day of the last battle of the gods, when Frey would sorely miss his faithful sword which he had given to Skirnir.

10

HOW FENRIS WOLF WAS BOUND

I T IS TRUE that Loki lived among the gods and was the foster brother of Odin. But he came from the race of the giants and he kept within his heart their crafty and evil ways.

When Loki lived with the giants he had a wife whose name was Angrboda. They had three children who were as fierce and terrible as their mother. The first was Fenris Wolf, the second was the Midgard Serpent, and the third was Hela.

Many years passed before the gods knew that these children of Loki lived among the giants. When Odin learned of it he feared that they might bring misfortune to the gods. Nothing but evil could be expected from them. So Odin ordered that they be brought to Asgard.

When Loki's children were brought before him Odin straightway cast the serpent into the sea. There, as the years went on, he grew so large that his body encircled the whole earth and he held his tail in his mouth.

Odin cast Hela into Niflheim and made her ruler over the nine worlds of the dead. Heroes who died a noble death in battle were carried to Valhalla. Those who died of sickness or old age or from other causes were to abide with Hela. They would dwell in her misty realm, guarded by high walls and great gates.

Odin allowed Fenris Wolf to remain in Asgard where the gods might keep watch over him. He was so fierce that only Tyr dared to give him meat. The gods became alarmed when they saw how the Wolf grew stronger each day. And they remembered that the prophecies all declared that in the end the Wolf would destroy the gods. Some plan must be made to keep Fenris Wolf in their power.

The gods made a strong chain. They brought it to the Wolf.

"Are you strong enough to break an iron chain?" they asked.

The Wolf looked at the chain.

"You may bind me with the chain," said the Wolf, thinking it no match for his strength.

The gods bound him carefully and tightly. But the fetter broke the first time the Wolf lashed out against it. The Wolf was soon free again.

Then the gods made a second chain twice as strong as the first. They took this to the Wolf.

"This chain is twice as strong as the other," they said. "You would indeed become famed for your strength if you could break this one."

The Wolf looked at the chain and saw how strong it was and with what skilled workmanship it had been made. Yet he thought his own strength had increased since he broke the first fetter. And it also came into his mind that he must risk danger if he would win fame.

"You may bind me with the chain," said the Wolf.

When the gods thought they had bound the chain as securely as possible, they said they were ready. The Wolf shook himself, dashed the fetter against the earth and struggled fiercely with it. He thrashed this way and that, putting all his strength against the chain. It broke and the fragments flew far off.

When these two attempts failed the gods feared they should never be able to bind the Wolf.

At last Odin thought of a plan. He sent Skirnir, Frey's messenger, down into the region of the Dark Elves. Skirnir went to certain dwarfs, long famed for their skill, and they made for him a strange and wondrous fetter. It was made of six things: the noise a cat makes in walking, the beard of a woman, the roots of a rock, the sinews of a bear, the breath of a fish, and the spittle of a bird.

These are strange things indeed and you must wonder how a chain could be made of them. But there is proof that these things were used, for no sound comes from the footfall of a cat, a woman has no beard, and there are no roots beneath a rock. So all I have told you is true, though there are some things which cannot be put to the test.

When the dwarfs were finished the fetter was soft and smooth as a silken ribbon, but stronger than bands of iron.

Skirnir brought the fetter to the gods and they thanked him well for having done the errand. Then the gods took the Wolf to an island which lay in the midst of a lake. When they had reached the island they showed the Wolf the silken ribbon. The gods passed it among themselves and each tested its strength with his hands. The fetter did not break.

"You see it is somewhat stouter than it appears from its thickness," they said to Fenris Wolf. "But *you* could break it."

"As to the matter of this ribbon," said the Wolf, "it is so slender a band that it seems to me I shall get little glory even though I break it. Yet if it is made with cunning and trickery, no matter how small and slight it seems, I will never let it bind my feet."

The gods answered that the Wolf could easily tear apart a slight silken band, since he had broken great fetters of iron.

"But if you are not able to burst this band," they said, "you will not be able to threaten the gods and we will set you free."

"Once I am bound," said the Wolf, "it will be a long time before I am free if I must wait your help. I am unwilling to have this bond put upon me. Yet rather than you should doubt my courage, let one of

you lay his hand in my mouth, for a pledge that the thing is done in good faith."

Each of the gods looked at his neighbor and none was willing to risk his hand. Then Tyr stretched out his right hand and laid it in the Wolf's mouth.

The gods bound the Wolf with the silken fetter. But when the Wolf would set himself free and lashed out against it, the fetter hardened. The more he struggled the tighter the bonds became. All the gods laughed except Tyr. Tyr lost his hand.

When the gods saw that the Wolf was bound and helpless, they fastened a chain to the fetter and passed the chain around a great rock. Then they put the rock into the ground and with a huge stone drove it deep down into the earth, and laid the stone over it.

The Wolf snarled and snapped his jaws. He struggled in the bonds and strove to bite the gods. So they thrust a sword into his mouth to hold his jaws apart.

And there he lay securely bound, until the day of the last battle of the gods.

11

THOR'S COMBAT WITH RUNGNIR

N O ONE but the giant Rungnir ever challenged Thor to single combat and he had cause to regret his daring. It came about in this way:

One day Thor was gone into the east to do battle with the trolls. While Thor was away Odin rode forth from Asgard upon his mighty eight-footed horse Sleipnir. He rode all the way to Jotunheim and there he met the giant who was named Rungnir.

"Who are you who wears a golden helmet and can ride through air and water?" Rungnir called to him. "Yours must be a wondrous steed to come so far."

Odin answered that he would wager his head that no horse in Jotunheim would prove as good.

"Well," said Rungnir, "no doubt yours is a good horse but it is not the best horse there is. I have a far swifter horse which is called Gold-Mane."

When Odin rode off without replying Rungnir

became angry. He leaped upon his horse Gold-Mane and galloped after Odin, thinking to show him which was the better horse.

Odin galloped so furiously that he was on top of the next hill first and he was still ahead at the top of the next one. Rungnir galloped after Odin, striving with such frenzy to overtake him that he forgot where he was. Before he knew it he had followed Odin within the gates of Asgard.

The gods show hospitality even to an enemy. They invited Rungnir within the hall to have meat and drink. The flagons were brought from which Thor drank and Rungnir emptied each in turn. When he had drunk more ale than was good for him he began to boast and use big words about what he could do.

"I will lift up Valhalla and carry it off to Jotunheim," shouted Rungnir. "I will level Asgard to the earth and destroy the gods. Only Freyja and Sif shall be saved and I will carry them home with me."

He shouted and boasted and declared he would drink up all the ale of the gods. None but Freyja dared pour his mead for him.

At length the gods grew tired of his noise and talk. They sent for Thor.

Thor came into the hall, swinging his hammer and angry that Rungnir should dare to be there.

"Who has allowed Rungnir safe-conduct in Valhalla," shouted Thor. "Who says he can sit at the table of the gods? Why does Freyja wait upon him as though he were one of us?"

Rungnir looked at Thor with unfriendly eyes and answered that he was under Odin's safe-conduct.

"It is All-Father himself who has invited me to drink in Valhalla," cried Rungnir.

"Be it so," said Thor. "But before you leave you will wish you had not come."

Rungnir replied that Thor would gain little renown if he killed him now, when he had no weapons.

"They will call you coward," cried Rungnir. "It would be a greater trial of courage if you would dare to fight with me on the border of Jotunheim. I was a fool to bring no weapons. If I had them we should try single combat. As matters stand now, I declare you a coward if you slay me, a weaponless man."

Thor was ready enough to accept Rungnir's challenge, for no one had ever before offered to fight him in single combat.

Then Rungnir went on his way. He galloped as hard as he could until he came to Jotunheim. The news of his journey was soon spread among the giants and it became known that a meeting had been arranged between Rungnir and Thor. The giants knew they had much at stake in this battle. Rungnir was the strongest of all the giants. If he perished their loss would be great.

So the giants made a man of clay to help Rungnir.

He was nine miles high and three miles broad across the chest. They could find no heart big enough to fit him, until they took one from a mare.

Rungnir was famous for his heart because it was made of hard stone and had three sharp corners. His head also was hard as stone. His shield, too, was stone, wide and thick. He held the shield before him and went forth to wait for Thor. He had a flintstone, which he flung over his shoulders, for a weapon. He was not a pretty sight. At his side stood the clay giant.

Thor went forth from Asgard to the place which had been arranged. Thjalfi went with him. Thjalfi ran ahead to the spot where Rungnir stood.

"You stand unwarily, Giant, holding your shield before you," he said. "Thor has seen you and he comes toward you under the earth. He will come at you from below."

When Rungnir heard this he thrust his shield under his feet and stood upon it. He took his flintstone in both hands and swung it above his head.

The lightning flashed and great claps of thunder shook the earth. Rungnir saw Thor coming toward him. Thor strode forward, filled with his godlike strength and anger. He swung his hammer with all his might and cast it at Rungnir from afar off. At the same moment Rungnir cast his flintstone against Thor. It struck the hammer in its flight and the flintstone burst into pieces. One part fell to the earth and from it have come all the rocks of flint. The other part struck Thor and lodged in his forehead so that he fell forward to the earth. But the hammer Mjollnir had struck the giant in the middle of the head and smashed his skull to bits. Rungnir fell forward upon Thor and one foot lay across Thor's neck.

In the meantime, Thjalfi fought with the clay giant and had little trouble in overcoming him.

Then Thjalfi went over to Thor and tried to lift Rungnir's foot from him, but he had not sufficient strength to move it. When the gods heard the outcome of the battle they came forth also, but not one of them could move Rungnir's foot. Then Magni, who was Thor's son, came forward. He was then but three days old. With ease he lifted the foot from Thor's neck.

"It is too bad, Father, that I came so late," said Magni. "I would have struck this giant dead with one blow of my fist had I met with him."

Thor rose up and welcomed his son. "It is clearly to be seen that in time you will amount to something," he said. "And I will give you the horse Gold-Mane, which Rungnir possessed."

Thor went home to Thrudvangar, but the flint-stone remained sticking in his head. He sought the aid of a wise woman who was called Groa, the wife of Aurvandill the Valiant. Groa sang her spells over Thor until the stone was loosened. When Thor knew that the stone was loose and there was hope that it might be removed, he wanted to reward Groa for her skill. So he told her some things that he knew would make her glad.

He told Groa how he had rescued her husband from the giants. Thor had waded across the Icy Stream, with Aurvandill hidden in a basket on his back, and so brought him safely from the north out of Jotunheim. As proof of his story, Thor said that one of Aurvandill's toes had stuck out of the basket and become frozen. Thor broke off the toe and cast it up into the heavens and made there the star called Aurvandill's Toe.

"It will not be long before Aurvandill returns home again," said Thor.

Groa was so happy at this news that she forgot her spells. No matter how she tried she could not recall them again. So the stone remained in Thor's head. And afterward it was always forbidden to throw a flintstone across the floor, for this caused the stone in Thor's head to move and gave the god great discomfort.

12

THE APPLES OF IDUNA

ODIN OFTEN TRAVELED forth from Asgard to take part in the affairs of men and to see what was going on in all the wide expanses of the world. One day he set out on such a journey, taking Loki and Hoenir with him. They wandered a long way over mountains and waste land and at length they grew hungry. But food was hard to find in that lonely country.

They had walked many miles when they saw a herd of oxen grazing in a valley.

"There is food for us at last," said Hoenir.

They went down into the valley and it was not long before they had one of the oxen roasting on a fire. While their meal cooked they stretched out on the ground to rest. When they thought the meat had cooked long enough they took it off the fire. But it was not yet ready. So they put it back over the embers and waited.

"I can wait no longer," cried Loki at last. "I am starving. Surely the meat is ready."

The gods scattered the fire once more and pulled forth the ox, but it seemed as though it had not even begun to cook. It was certainly not fit for eating.

This was a strange thing and not even Odin knew the meaning of it. As they wondered among themselves, they heard a voice speak from the great oak tree above them.

"It is because of me," said the voice, "that there is no virtue in your fire and your meat will not cook."

They looked up into the branches of the tree and there sat a huge eagle.

"If you are willing to give me a share of the ox, then it will cook in the fire," said the eagle.

There was little the gods could do but agree to this. The eagle let himself float down from the tree and alighted by the fire. In no time at all the ox was roasted. At once the eagle took to himself the two hindquarters and the two forequarters as well.

This greediness angered Loki. He snatched up a great pole, brandished it with all his strength, and struck the eagle with it. The eagle plunged violently at the blow and whirled into the air. One end of the pole stuck fast to the eagle's back and Loki's hands

stuck fast to the other end. No matter how he tried he could not free them. Swooping and turning, the eagle dragged Loki after him in his flight, flying just low enough that Loki's feet and legs knocked against stones and rock heaps and trees. Loki thought his arms would be torn from his shoulders. He cried out for mercy.

"Put me down! Put me down!" begged Loki. "Free me and you shall have the whole ox for your own."

"I do not want the ox," cried the eagle. "I want only one thing—Iduna and her apples. Deliver them into my power and I will set you free."

Iduna was the beautiful and beloved wife of the god Bragi. She guarded the most precious possession of the gods, the apples of youth. Unless they might eat of them the gods would grow old and feeble like mortal men. They kept the gods ever young. Iduna and her apples were priceless beyond words.

"Iduna and her apples! Such a thing cannot be done," shouted Loki.

"Then I will fly all day," screamed the eagle. "I will knock you against the rocks until you die." And he dragged Loki through rough tree branches and against the sides of mountains and over the rocky earth. Loki could endure it no longer.

"I will do as you ask," he cried. "I will bring Iduna to you, and her apples as well."

"Give me your oath," said the eagle. Loki gave his

oath. A time was set when Loki should put Iduna in the eagle's power.

The eagle straightway made Loki free and flew off into the sky. A much-bruised Loki returned to his companions and all three set off on their homeward journey. But Odin and Hoenir did not know the promise which Loki had made.

Loki pondered how he could keep his word to the eagle, whom he now knew to be the giant Thjazi in disguise. When the appointed day came Loki approached Iduna.

"Iduna," he said, speaking gently, "yesterday I found a tree on which grow wondrous apples. It is in the wood to the north of Asgard. They are like your apples in color and shape. Surely they must have the same properties. Should we not gather them and bring them to Asgard?"

"There are no apples anywhere," said Iduna, "like to my apples."

"These are," said Loki. "They are very like. Come and look for yourself. If you bring your apples we can put them side by side and you will see."

So Iduna went with Loki to the wood, taking her apples with her. While they were in the wood the giant Thjazi swooped down in his eagle's plumage and carried Iduna and her apples off to his abode.

The gods soon missed Iduna. And they knew her apples were gone, for the signs of old age began to show among them. They grew bent and stiff and stooped.

Odin called a hasty council of the gods. They asked each other what they knew of Iduna.

"Where was she last seen?" asked Odin.

Heimdal had seen her walking out of Asgard with Loki. That was the last that was known of her.

Odin sent Thor to seize Loki and to bring him to the council. When Loki was brought the gods threatened him with tortures and death unless he told what he knew of Iduna. Loki grew frightened and admitted that Iduna had been carried off to Jotunheim.

"I will go in search of her," he cried, "if Freyja will lend me her falcon wings."

Freyja was more than willing. When Loki had put on the feather dress he flew to the north in the direction of Jotunheim.

He flew for a long time before he came to the home of Thjazi, the giant. Then he circled slowly overhead and saw Iduna walking below. She carried in her arms her golden casket of apples. Thjazi was nowhere to be seen, for he had rowed out to sea to fish. Loki quickly alighted on the ground beside Iduna.

"Hasten, Iduna," he cried, "I will rescue you." And he changed Iduna into the shape of a nut and flew off with her in his claws.

Loki had no sooner gone than Thjazi arrived home. At once he missed Iduna and her precious apples.

Putting on his eagle's plumage, he flew into the air. Far off in the distance he saw the falcon flying. Instantly he took after him. The eagle's wings beat powerfully, making a deep rushing sound like a great wind. Thjazi drew nearer and nearer to Loki. Loki flew with all his might, but the eagle was bearing down upon the falcon just as the towers of Asgard came into view. With a last burst of strength Loki hastened toward the shining battlements.

The gods were on watch for Loki's return. They saw the falcon bearing the nut between his claws, with the eagle in close pursuit. Quickly they built a great pile of wood shavings just outside the wall of Asgard. As Loki came near he swooped down low over the shavings. Thjazi swooped down too, hoping to seize the falcon before he reached the safety of Asgard. Just as the eagle came close to the pile the gods set fire to the shavings. Instantly the fire blazed up, but Thjazi could not stop himself. He plunged into the flames and the feathers of his wings took fire. Then he could fly no more and the gods slew him where he was.

There was great rejoicing within the walls of Asgard to have Iduna safe once more. And the gods grew young and bright again.

13

THE DEATH OF BALDER

BALDER WAS THE FAIREST and most beloved of all the gods. He was wise in judgment, gracious in speech, and all his deeds were pure and good. Wherever Balder went there was joy and warmth and gladness. He was beloved by gods and men, and so beautiful that the whitest flower which grew on the hillside was named "Balder's Brow."

It came about that Balder dreamed great and perilous dreams touching his life. Night after night they troubled his sleep. When Balder spoke of these dreams to the other gods they were filled with foreboding. They knew some danger threatened him and all the gods took counsel together as to how they might save Balder. They came to this decision: they would ask safety for Balder from every kind of danger.

Frigg, who was the mother of Balder, went to all things in the world to ask their help. Fire and water, stones, earth, and trees, iron and metal of all kinds, birds, beasts, and even serpents promised they would not harm Balder.

When the gods knew that Balder was safe they made up a game which they took delight in playing. Balder would stand in a circle of the gods and they would strike at him or hurl stones or cast missiles of one kind or another. But Balder stood unhurt in the midst of it all. And this seemed to the gods a wondrous thing, full of awe.

Loki alone was not pleased that Balder took no hurt. His evil, crafty mind began to plot against Balder the Good. Loki made himself appear like an old woman and in this likeness he went to the dwelling of Balder's mother. He greeted Frigg and she asked him if he knew what the gods were doing at their assembly.

"The gods have a new game. Balder stands before them and they hurl weapons of every kind at him," answered Loki, speaking with the voice of an old woman. "It is a strange thing that nothing harms him."

"Nothing will harm Balder, neither weapons nor rocks nor trees," said Frigg. "I have taken oaths of them all."

"Have all things taken oaths to spare Balder?" asked the old woman.

"All things save one," said Frigg. "A small tree-sprout grows west of Valhalla. It is called Mistletoe. I thought it too young a thing to be bound by an oath."

Immediately the old woman went away. Loki changed himself into his own shape and went west of Valhalla. He tore up the Mistletoe by the roots and carried it to where the gods were assembled.

Hod, the brother of Balder, took no part in the game because he was blind. He stood outside the ring of men.

Loki spoke to him. "Why do you not shoot at Balder?"

"I cannot see where Balder stands, nor have I any weapons," answered Hod.

Then Loki said: "You should do as the others do and show Balder honor. I will show you where he stands. Shoot at him with this wand."

Hod took the Mistletoe wand and shot at Balder, and Loki guided his hand.

The shaft flew through Balder and he fell dead to the earth. This was the greatest mischance that had ever befallen gods and men.

When Balder fell to the earth the gods could not speak a word for grief and anguish, nor could they move to lift him where he lay. Each looked at the other and they were all of one mind whose evil hand had done this deed. Yet they could take no revenge for they stood on hallowed ground.

When they tried to speak the tears came and the gods wept bitterly for the loss of Balder. They had no words with which to name their sorrow. Of them all Odin grieved most, for he understood best how great was the loss which had come to the gods.

The mother of Balder was the first to speak. "If any among you," said Frigg, "would win all my love and favor, let him ride the road to Hela's realm and seek Balder among the dead. Let him offer Hela a ransom if she will but let Balder come home to Asgard."

Hermod the Bold undertook the perilous journey. The great eight-footed horse of Odin, named Sleipnir, was brought forth. Hermod mounted and sped at once upon his way.

The gods took the body of Balder and brought it down to the sea, where Balder's ship was drawn up upon the shore. The gods wished to launch the ship and build Balder's funeral pyre upon it, but they could not move it from its place.

Then Odin sent for the giantess Hyrrokin, famed for her strength. She thrust the boat into the waters with such might that fire burst from the rollers beneath it and the earth trembled.

When the funeral pyre had been built, the body of Balder was borne to the ship. When his wife, Nanna, saw it her heart broke with grief and she died. The gods, with sorrow, laid her body beside Balder. The

fire was kindled. Thor stood near. With a sad heart
he lifted his hammer above the blaze and hallowed
the flames.

People of many races came to the burning. First of
all was Odin. His two ravens flew above him and
Frigg was by his side. The Valkyries were also with
him. Frey rode in his chariot drawn by his boar called
Gold-Mane and Freyja drove her cats. Then came the
other gods and goddesses. Many from the lands of the
Frost-Giants and the Hill-Giants were there also. All
grieved for Balder.

Odin laid upon the fire his ring which was called
Draupnir, from which every ninth night dropped
eight gold rings like to itself. The flames from the
funeral ship rose on high, shining in the air and on
the waters. The hearts of the gods were heavy with
grief as they watched the burning.

Meanwhile Hermod was on his way to Hela. He
rode nine nights through valleys so dark and deep
that he could see nothing. At length he came to the
river Gjoll. He rode on to the bridge which is paved
with glittering gold and guarded by the maiden
Modgud. She asked Hermod his name and from what
country and people he came.

"Only yesterday," she said, "five companies of
dead men crossed this bridge. But today it thunders as
much under you riding alone. Nor have you the pallor
of death. Why come you this way?"

"I have been sent to seek Balder among the dead," Hermod answered. "Has Balder passed this road?"

The maiden answered that Balder had crossed the bridge. "The way lies downward and to the north," she said.

Hermod rode on until he came to the wall of Hela's realm. He got down from his horse and made the girths of the saddle tight. Then he mounted again and pricked the horse with his spurs. In one great leap Sleipnir cleared the gates.

Hermod rode to the great hall where the dead were gathered. He dismounted and went inside. There he saw Balder sitting in the place of honor. Hermod stayed through the night. When morning came he begged Hela that Balder might ride home with him.

"The gods are desolate without him," said Hermod. "Every being in the world longs for his return."

Hela answered that it should be put to a test whether Balder were so greatly beloved.

"If all things in the world, living and dead, weep for him," said Hela, "he shall go back to Asgard and the gods. But if there is one thing which bears him no love and will not weep, Balder must remain with me."

When Hermod rose to leave, Balder went with him out of the hall. Balder gave the ring Draupnir to Hermod and asked that he take it to Odin for a remembrance. Nanna, Balder's wife, sent Frigg a linen smock and other gifts.

Hermod rode back and came to Asgard. He told all that he had seen and heard. Then the gods sent messengers all over the world to ask all things to weep for Balder, that he might return to them. All wept for Balder: men, and all living things; the earth and stones and trees, and every kind of metal. In the early morning you can still see their tears when the dew lies upon the grass.

As the messengers came home, their work well done, they found an old woman sitting by a cave. They asked her, as they had asked all others, to weep tears that Balder might come forth from the place of the dead. But she answered:

"I will weep no tears for Balder. I loved him not. Let Hela keep what she holds. Let her keep what she holds."

And because one out of all the world would not weep for the god, Balder must stay where he was. Gods and men knew that this again was Loki's evil work. This time he must pay the price for all that he had done. The gods revenged themselves on Loki. But Balder remained with Hela, and the earth was never again as fair to gods or men.

14

THE PUNISHMENT OF LOKI

T HE GODS did not forgive Loki. Deep in their
hearts they knew who had brought about the
death of Balder and whose evil had kept Balder within Hela's gates. But while Loki remained within the
hallowed ground of Asgard he was safe from their
revenge.

Loki pursued his old ways. He taunted and defied
the gods until one day Thor could stand it no longer.

"Hold your tongue, Loki!" he cried, raising his
hammer. "Hold your tongue, or I will strike you dead
where you stand."

Then Loki grew fearful. He knew the gods scorned
him and Thor longed to destroy him. He fled from
Asgard and made himself a hiding place deep in the
mountains. Here he built a house with four doors.
Each side of the house had a door so that he might
look out in all directions. Loki knew the gods would

try to find where he was hidden and he would need all his wiles to escape them. Often he would change into the likeness of a salmon and swim in the great river that flowed near his door.

One day as he was swimming he wondered what sort of thing the gods could make to catch him in the river. When he went back to his house he amused himself by taking linen twine and tying it together in meshes, in the fashion in which a fisherman's net has been made ever since.

Meanwhile far off in Asgard the gods were plotting how they might take Loki. Odin sat down in his high seat from whence he could look out over all the world. He searched the valleys and the seas and the mountains. At last he saw where Loki had hidden himself. Then the gods went forth against Loki.

Loki was sitting before his fire making his net larger. When he saw the gods coming he threw the net into the fire and ran to the river. At once he dived into the water, changing into a salmon.

When the gods reached Loki's house Kvasir, who was known for his wisdom, was the first to enter. As soon as Kvasir saw in the fire the white ash where the net had burned he understood that this was something to be used for catching fish. Then the gods knew that Loki must have changed himself into a fish and was hiding in the river.

"Ah," cried Thor, "we will catch him with his own tricks!"

So the gods took more cord and set to work to make a net. They tied the twine in meshes, following the pattern of the burnt-out ashes of Loki's net. When it was ready they went to the river and cast the net into the water. Thor took hold of one end and the other gods held up the other end. There was a mighty waterfall in the river and they cast the net near the foot of it and dragged it toward the sea. As they came near to him Loki lay quiet between two stones on the bottom of the river. The net passed over him. But the gods saw that something moved in front of the net.

A second time they went up to the waterfall and cast in the net. This time they tied stones in it so that it would sink and nothing could pass under it. Loki swam ahead of the net, until he saw that it was but a short distance to the sea. With a mighty leap he jumped out of the water and over the net and swam back to the waterfall.

This time the gods saw where Loki hid. They divided into two companies, each holding one end of the net. Thor plunged into midstream and waded behind the net as the gods drew it toward the sea. Loki saw that he had only two choices. It would be a great risk of his life to be carried out to sea . . . the one thing left was to leap over the net once more. With all his strength Loki gave a great leap into the

air. But now Thor was waiting for him. Thor clutched at Loki as he jumped and his great hand closed on the salmon's back. The wet fish slipped in Thor's fingers but Thor squeezed hard and held on. This is the reason that the back of a salmon grows narrow toward the tail.

Thus Loki was taken captive outside the bounds of any hallowed place. He need expect no mercy. On dry land he changed into his own shape and the gods carried him to a cavern deep within the mountains. They took three flat stones and bored a hole in each stone. They bound Loki over the stones with bonds that turned to iron. Then they took a serpent and fastened it up over him, so that the venom should drip from the serpent into Loki's face. And there the gods left him.

Only Loki's wife, Sigyn, remained faithful to him. She stood beside him and caught the drops of venom in a basin. But when the basin was full she must turn aside to empty it. Then the venom drops upon Loki. He writhes against it with such force that the whole earth trembles. But Loki must lie in these bonds till that last day when the gods shall be overcome in battle.

15
THE NEW DAY

LOKI LAY in his bonds until the day when the last battle of the gods drew near. The wise Odin, and Frigg, and all who understood the prophecies, knew that the world of the gods would not last forever. The death of Balder hastened the day of doom. Beauty and innocence were gone from the earth. Violence and all the ways of evil increased. Brother fought against brother, and son against father.

Sunlight and warmth grew less on the earth. There came three years like one long winter, when bitter winds blew from every quarter and snow piled in great drifts. The sun and the moon were darkened in the heavens and the stars were quenched. Earth and all the mountains trembled; trees were uprooted and all bonds were burst asunder.

Loki was free to work his evil will and Fenris Wolf escaped his shackles. The Midgard Serpent rose from the depths of the sea. The waters, lashed into turmoil, washed over the earth. Streams overflowed their banks, lakes had no shores, and the sea spread through valleys and covered mountains.

Fire was abroad on the earth. The giant Surt rode forth from the south, all the sons of Muspellheim in his wake, with flame burning before him and behind him.

The Frost-Giants and Hill-Giants came forth in all their might. Together with Surt and Loki and all the evil forces of the world they hurled themselves on the bridge Bifrost. It broke beneath their weight; but they had crossed into Asgard.

Heimdal blew his Gjallar-Horn in warning, and its echoes rang through all the worlds. The gods' cock, with the golden comb, crowed to waken the heroes that they might fight by the side of Odin and the gods.

Gods and heroes donned their armor and marched to the fields of Vigrid. Odin rode foremost, his golden helmet and byrnie gleaming. Thor strode at his side. They hurled themselves against their foes and the turmoil of battle rose. On every hand were fierce encounters. But fate was against the gods.

Fenris Wolf destroyed Odin. Thor could give no help for he struggled against the Midgard Serpent. Thor killed the Serpent, but when he had walked eight paces he fell dead, slain by the Serpent's venom. Loki and Heimdal killed each other. Frey fought with

Surt and was overcome. Then he could have used well that good sword which he gave to Skirnir.

The gods were doomed. The day of their last battle had come. Yggdrasil, the tree of the universe, trembled and all things in heaven and earth were filled with dread.

Yet, as was told in the prophecies, this was not the end. After darkness and silence, a new day came. Out of the sea arose a new earth, green and fair, whose fields bore harvest without the sowing of seed. A new sun, daughter of the old, shone in the heavens, even more beautiful than her mother. All the ancient evil was passed and gone. Balder was again among the living, and light and beauty returned to the earth.

Those gods who remained made their dwelling again where Asgard had stood. In the grass they found scattered the gold chessmen with which they once played, and they remembered together the vanished past and the days of Thor and Odin.

A new race of men walked the earth; goodness and happiness were their portion. Halls roofed with gold, more fair than the sun, rose among the clouds. And all awaited the coming of the Mighty One, he who should govern all things.

NOTE ON THE NORSE MYTHS

THERE was a time when the gods about whom the stories in this book are told were very real to the men who lived in northern Europe. They heard in the stormy sky the mighty thunder of Thor's chariot; they loved the good and beautiful Balder; they gave praise and worship to the all-wise Odin. Those days now seem to us to belong to a vague and distant past. Yet it was our past and those men among the founders of our race. Even today the names of four days of our week are taken from the names of these same Norse gods—Tuesday, Wednesday, Thursday, and Friday. That past seems less remote when we remember this.

It is to the small, remarkable country of Iceland that we especially owe the preservation of these stories. There they were written down, after having been told for centuries and passed from generation to generation. They were collected in what we now call the Poetic Edda and the Prose Edda, or the Elder Edda and the Younger Edda. The Poetic Edda is a collection of anonymous poems. The Prose Edda was compiled by Snorri Sturluson. By the time the stories were recorded the beliefs of Christianity had begun to make their way into that far northern world and the old gods were no longer worshiped as deities, though the stories of their great deeds were still told and treasured.

Snorri Sturluson gives this advice to the young skalds or poets for whose guidance he wrote the Prose Edda:

"Young skalds, who desire to attain to the craft of poetry, must seek to use these tales as the Chief Skalds have used them. Christian men need not believe in pagan gods; yet are these tales to be revered as ancient tradition, neither to be believed in nor to be tampered with."

The Norse myths are the tales of adventure and wisdom and pity and folly and beauty with which the early men of the North tried to explain the mystery of their world, and to put down the great exploits of the gods who ruled their heaven and earth. In the present re-telling the author has tried to follow Snorri's advice to young skalds, and to treat the tales with affection and respect and understanding.

This adaptation has depended chiefly upon the following for source material:

The Poetic Edda. Tr. Henry Adams Bellows. New York, The American-Scandinavian Foundation, 1923.

The Prose Edda. By Snorri Sturluson. Tr. Arthur Gilchrist Brodeur. New York, The American-Scandinavian Foundation, 1916.

Norse Mythology. By Peter Andreas Munch. Revision of Magnus Olsen. Tr. Sigurd Bernhard Hustvedt. New York, The American-Scandinavian Foundation, 1927.

PRONUNCIATION OF PROPER NAMES

THE proper names in the Norse myths may be found with various spellings and authorities do not always agree as to the best way to pronounce them. This list of names has been marked as simply as possible to give an approximate pronunciation.

The marked vowels should be pronounced as in the following words: fāte, fäther, bē, mĕt, admĭt, hōld, spŏt, foŏt, moōn, pūre.

Aegir	ĕ' gir
Angrboda	än' gĕr bō dä
Asgard	äs' gärd
Ask	äsk
Audhumla	oud' hoōm lä
Aurvandill	our' vän dil
Balder	bäl' der
Banir	bä' nir
Baugi	bou' gē
Beli	bĕl' i
Bergelmir	bĕr' gĕl mir
Bifrost	bēf' rŏst
Bolverk	boōl' verk
Borr	boŏr
Buri	boō' ri
Draupnir	droup' nir
Egil	ā' gĕl
Elli	ĕl' lē
Embla	ĕm' blä
Fenris Wolf	fĕn' ris wolf
Fjalar	fyäl' är
Frey	frā

Freyja	frā′ yä
Frigg	frĭg
Galarr	gäl′ är
Gerd	gĕrd
Gilling	gĭl′ ling
Gjallar-Horn	yäl′ lär horn
Gjol	yōl
Gladsheim	gläds′ hām
Groa	grō′ a
Gungnir	gŏong′ nir
Gunlod	gŏon′ lŏd
Gymir	gē′ mir
Heimdal	hām′ däl
Hela	hĕl′ ä
Hermod	hĕr′ mōd
Hod	hōd
Hoenir	hē′ nir
Hugi	hū′ gē
Hymir	hē′ mir
Hyrrokin	hĕr′ ro kin
Iduna	ē′ dōon a
Ivaldi	ē′ väld i
Jotun	yō′ tŏon
Jotunheim	yō′ tŏon hām
Kvasir	kvä′ sir
Logi	lō′ gē
Loki	lō′ kē
Magni	mäg′ nē
Midgard	mĭd′ gärd
Mimir	mē′ mir
Mjollnir	myŏl′ nir
Modgud	mŏod′ gŏod
Muspellheim	mŏos′ pĕl hām
Nanna	nän′ nä
Nidhogg	nēd′ hŏg
Niflheim	nĭfl′ hām
Odin	ō′ din
Ratatosk	rä′ tä tosk
Roskva	rŏsk′ va
Rungnir	rŏong′ nir
Sif	sĭf
Sigyn	sĭ′ gin

Sindri	sĭn′ drē
Skidbladnir	skēd′ bläd nir
Skirnir	skĭr′ nir
Skrymir	skrē′ mir
Sleipnir	slāp′ nir
Surt	sōort
Suttung	sōot′ tōong
Svadilfari	sväd′ il fä ri
Thjalfi	thyäl′ fē
Thjazi	thyät′ sē
Thor	thor
Thrudvangar	thrōōd′ väng ar
Thrym	thrĭm
Tyr	tēr
Urd	ōōrd
Utgard-Loki	ōōt′ gärd lō′ kē
Valhalla	văl′ hăl a
Valkyrie	văl′ kĭr ĭ
Vanir	vä′ nir
Ve	vā
Vigrid	vĭg′ rid
Vili	vē′ lē
Yggdrasil	ĭg′ drä sil
Ymir	ē′ mir